DRIVIN

Safe and Res|

INDEPENDENCE

John P Brown   (Cert. Ed. Cert. Sp. Ed. ADI)
Specialist Teacher and Disability Driving Instructor

Published by: Driving is: Publications. 6 BH21 2SR
Printed by: Think Ink, (01473) 400162
ISBN   978-0-9558282-5-6

CONTENTS

Page

Introduction

-I have been asked to write this book following the introduction of Independent Driving to help both Instructors and Examiners to become more **aware** of the new challenges that are now facing those with 'Hidden Difficulties'. I trust these guidance notes will assist those with limited **knowledge** of the various problems to **understand** how some clients experience ID and to **care** about why they may be being disadvantaged if inappropriate methods are being used. It is a follow up to my previous books: I have tried not to repeat anything already written although the themes and facts are obviously similar.

BOOK 1 'Driving is more about Psychology than Systems' (ISBN 978-0-9558282-1-8) in which I consider the different factors to be taken into account as we choose the methods of teaching most applicable to those clients who may be struggling. I have approached this from the viewpoint of the <u>learner</u> rather than the instructor and have deliberately avoided any set methods or those which may be in vogue at any specific time. I have discussed what I call <u>Developmental Driving</u> where we aim to tailor our lessons to the need and the level of our individual clients and in order to develop their skills, begin at <u>their</u> level of ability rather than at our predetermined level of prescribed instruction.

BOOK 2 'Driving is turning Disability into Ability' (ISBN 978-0-9558282-3-2) in which I describe various conditions and disabilities and refer to the case histories of those with problems whom I have successfully taught to drive and look at the positive changes that driving has made to their lives. I also discuss the many wide-ranging opportunities available for the more creative ADIs beyond teaching 'normal' teenage learners.
****

I know a number of you from the meetings at which I have spoken and from interaction on the various ADI forums. Feel free to use the individual chapters as a basis for discussion. If you wish for further information re any of the books then please refer to my web site www.drivingincludesu.co.uk or contact me at; inclusivedriving@yahoo.co.uk

Terminology

Special Needs (SN): a Generic description of any aspect of Physical, Mental, Emotional and Educational Difficulties.

Specific Needs (SpN): the term used for normally well-functioning people whose development may have varied from the norm, or who have experienced specific areas of difficulty which may make them perceive or behave differently and so need to learn in an alternative way which focuses and builds on their strengths.

Complex Needs: the term used to describe requirements which may be indicated in a number of different interrelated ways, but may have developed from one root cause. Dyslexia may be linked to ADHD and Aspergers may be linked with Dyspraxia, but through consequent frustration these may lead to socially unacceptable behaviour. The difficulty for teachers is to be able to work out what the underlying root cause is, rather than just reacting to what they are observing.

Specific Requirements: a term used to explain the appropriate support which would help balance the differences to make sure the clients are not disadvantaged and so are able to attain their natural potential.

Statement: the term used under the 1981 Education Act to describe the legal document which 'States' the requirements of children in education whose needs are severe enough to be assessed and to have special provision legally provided by the Local Education Committees.

Inclusion: this was the term used in the Warnock Report into Special Educational Needs of 1978 which meant that legally children with SN must be given the same educational opportunities. "Inclusion should mean being involved in a common enterprise of learning." This did not necessarily mean they had to be taught in the same way or even at the same level, but that they should be included and provided with all relevant opportunities, rather than being excluded because they were unable to attain success in the same way as their peers.

Differentiation: the term used to explain the different methods which must be used to help the student achieve the results they are capable of attaining. Differentiation can be divided into three sections.

1. **Content:**   through different ways of **Presentation.**
2. **Process:**   through employing different teaching **Methods.**
3. **Assessment:** through enabling them to demonstrate in different
               ways their new **Knowledge**.

It does not mean dumbing-down, but finding more appropriate methods to achieve the same level of success.

Spectrum The condition is so termed since there is a huge variation in both the manifestation and in the degree of effect and affect it can have. If mild and difficult to pin-point, then the term **tendencies** may also be used, e.g. Autistic Spectrum Disorder or Autistic Tendencies.

Who is Affected? 21% of the population will have some area of diagnosed Special Need, but only a few of those receive Statements so the majority will have **Hidden Disabilities.** At least half of those diagnosed will never be able to drive, nor would they expect to, but many more with undiagnosed Specific Needs will wish to learn and could become safe competent drivers. We can estimate that 20% who wish to learn to drive will have Specific Needs which should be understood and catered for. Many of those hidden difficulties will never have been identified, nor would the learner drivers wish to be categorised as having Special Needs.

Identified or Recognised? If it was suggested candidates had a SN they could be seriously insulted as many of them will have been academically capable and developed successful coping strategies or will have learnt to mask their problems. It would therefore be unwise to either ask them, or to imply they have a problem unless they volunteer the information, but it is still important that their needs are recognised and differentiation in both teaching and assessment is implemented.

-If they were given an option to use the methods they actually employ to drive independently and were given the choice to be assessed on their strengths, it would not devalue the integrity of the tests because the same knowledge would be being assessed, but by using different methods. The instructor needs to be sensitive to their client's needs and to work in partnership with them to develop their strengths and the examiner needs to understand their behaviour in order to correctly judge their driving ability.

Why do Examiners need to understand Complex Needs?

-In 2010 Independent Driving became an integral part of the British Driving Test. This created a contradiction in that driving independently had always been the method used by those with difficulties to enable them to drive <u>safely</u>, but when they were required to 'independently' drive according to a prescribed system they were put at a serious disadvantage.

-ID has undoubtedly been a success for those without problems, but it has severely affected some of those with Hidden Needs who have been forced to be tested on their weaknesses. This may not have been the intention, but instructors have observed the distraction caused and the potential danger created when misunderstandings are triggered. It has been especially so if the confusion is compounded by the examiner rushing subsequent instructions aimed at getting the candidate back on route. They would have been able to drive safely using the independent methods developed with their instructors, but often these were not allowed on test.

-The ten minutes of intense memory required to comprehend, recall, and then apply verbal instructions whilst also retaining visual sequences was for some too onerous and seeking route reinforcement was impossible. Prior to ID those with hidden difficulties had been able to rely on following given instructions, irrespective of whether the examiner either knew about, or understood their conditions, so the examining methods had been more conducive to both their safety and their success. The examiner had been in control, rather than needing to understand their strengths and weaknesses, how their mind functioned, or what they might do under strange requests and then be expected to cope with the results.

-As they were now being directed to perform in an unreal scenario, it compromised their ability to adapt and drive according to their own independent requirements, so the examiners and candidates now became at risk since both had lost control of their own situations and of the test. A further dilemma was that examiners should have been able to let them choose the methods they would naturally use, but to give that freedom was deemed unacceptable as it would affect the 'integrity of the test' and yet not to assess their true independence, actually destroyed the integrity of the test in relation to the individuals concerned.

-ADIs need to be able to explain the **effects** of their candidate's conditions when booking, rather than selecting a term from a set list which may be inappropriate or misleading. This process was rejected on the grounds of the expense of modifying the booking system, so examiners are required to have a deeper understanding of the many hidden disabilities categorised as Specific Needs and it is now recognised that they need further training to enable them to predict and understand the potential dangers in order to act appropriately when candidates are in ID mode.

-Initially it was stated that to give examiners time to deal with the care needed, all SNs candidates should be classed as 'disabled' and receive double slots. It was then realised this could in theory affect one in five tests and these are not only difficult to obtain for the candidate, but many do not want to be classed as having a 'disability,' especially if it is hidden.

-It is both insensitive and intrusive for examiners to have to ask about the effects of their conditions as they walk to the car, but the stated disabilities have sometimes misled examiners and left them actually having to question candidates about the effects before the test. This has obviously been inappropriate as candidates don't want to be talking to strangers about their medical history or psychological conditions when taking a Driving Test. The complexity of the condition is not relevant, but an understanding of the personal techniques required and how to assess any anomalies which may be manifest is essential.

-The situation has been further complicated by the fact that many candidates would not admit to their needs or had never even considered them as needs because they had subconsciously developed their own independent coping and avoidance strategies. It was only when they were faced with this form of ID that their problems came to the fore and they were taken out of their comfort zone and under the stress of test were asked to do what they were incapable of and what was unnecessary.

-It was like asking a paraplegic who had learnt to use hand controls to then be tested by using pedals. The immediate solution would be to provide all candidates with a choice of the method they would wish to use which they would select when booking and to educate examiners to understand the wider needs of what they observed.

Should ADIs Diagnose?

-I was contacted by an irate mother who asked me to assess and teach her daughter following her current instructor's diagnosis of 'autism.' I calmed her down by explaining that I believed her daughter may benefit from a different form of teaching and after giving a few pointers and directed help she soon began to enjoy her lessons and became a proficient driver without any sign of autistic traits.

-I have wondered whether ADIs may actually 'create' what can appear to be Special Needs when they teach in an inappropriate way for that particular client. It could be argued that Examiners can also 'create' failure if they do not recognise or understand the candidate's condition or the reasons which lie beneath the techniques they employ to assist their safe-driving: on the grounds of 'safety,' some examiners have refused the perfectly acceptable use of Post-it notes.

-Before any examiners or instructors think this is an attack on them, I can assure them that it is not and it is only my attempt to stimulate professional discussion to right a wrong which has developed. I deeply respect the examiners with whom I work as they are highly experienced and sympathetic to those with Specific Needs, but with more knowledge and training, some situations could be avoided.

- When applying for a test, what should be declared if the client does not know, or will not recognise, or wants to keep quiet that they have a Specific Need? ADIs are not medics and we should not be put in the position of having to diagnose, but for pragmatic reasons, that is what we often have to do. We should be able to state what they require, rather than diagnose a formal condition. So what indicators are instructors looking for and also how should Examiners identify the undeclared problems with which they are presented so that they do not disadvantage their clients?

-I taught a young dancer with Cerebral Palsy, but the booking department wanted to register her as having a mobility disability, rather than the manifest Information Processing problem. After 40 minutes on the phone they still could not understand the issues as IP was not on their list of disabilities, so we had to settle for Dyspraxia and a disability slot!! Is dyspraxia a physical disability or a sequential memory problem?

-What I wanted to be able to state was; 'This candidate will take time to understand your directions so please give them clearly and in good time to enable her to listen, comprehend and carry them out.' It is in the lap of the gods as to whether the examiner understands the significance of the declared conditions and I feel uncomfortable when they ask the candidate, *"you have declared a disability, so what modifications do you need to the car?"* In the mind of the candidate they have not declared a 'disability,' but only a difficulty which may require extra time and understanding.

-Since ID, examiners have been selecting the task they think is the most appropriate, rather than seeking from the candidate what they require and so mistakes have been made. There are those keen to learn about the difficulties who in a friendly way ask candidates about the effects of their conditions <u>as they drive along</u>. *"I am keen to know more because my friend's son has problems."* Not a good idea because of possible emotional distraction!

-Most of my referrals come following negative learning experiences so I ask, *"Why did you not tell your Instructor about your problem?"* The common answer is, <u>*"They did not ask."*</u> We must observe, ask and understand, but how do we find out the meaning to what we are observing and when the evidence is plain to see, do we actually understand the message being given and do we have the experience to deal with it?

-Some of the indications of a muddled brain are so clear if only we can interpret them. One example was cited on 'ADI Forum.' The instructor suspected that dyspraxia lay at the root of the difficulties a high achieving academic student was experiencing. Suspicions were reinforced when she stated her 'placement ran from October, September, August, July, June, May to April.' This was the final piece in the jig saw and even though the diagnosis was blatantly obvious, the student was offended when it was suggested she may have an underlying problem. It is sometimes even more difficult for high achievers to accept why they are struggling.

- My advice is that it is not advisable to formally diagnose, because we do not know, but that does not mean we should not recognise the effects that we are observing and so teach and examine accordingly. We cannot presume we will be told about any condition, but if we are then that is a bonus to help us act accordingly.

Identification Strategies

-It is essential that neither examiners nor instructors diagnose. That is not our job and we do not have the experience or the skills, nor do we know the background to understand the specific reasons why a condition has or has not been identified. The background could lie in the availability or provision of finances rather than of need, or in a family refusal to accept a given diagnosis. Our task as instructors is to build a picture through relaxed chat which can often be achieved by asking a few strategic questions: Which school did you go to? What subjects are you studying? What sports do you play? What are your interests? Do you ride a bike?

-When they know you are interested in them as people, rather than in what you are going to impart to them, then they will open up because they will trust you and you will get your answers and so be best able to teach them. If they are reserved and don't like chatting, then I just talk about life and what we are observing as we drive along and introduce leading topics and invariably they join in. Occasionally I have taught those with little voluntary speech, but that does not mean they cannot communicate.

-We do not need a formal diagnosis, but just relevant observations to help us discover how best to teach each individual, although it does help if we find there has been one written so we know what to say on the test application to ensure they receive a fair chance of success. ADIs are in a unique and privileged position to closely observe their client's behaviour and possibly for the first time help them understand and come to terms with problems they may have struggled with for all their lives. Their future education can now begin under the positive guidance of the ADI and the understanding care of the Examiner and hopefully a system which will allow them to function to their best.

-Instructors can have a huge impact on not only the individual, but indirectly on society in general. We are influential in changing the lives of some by halting their slide into unemployment and worthlessness and by changing their attitude to driving. The biggest danger on the road is not lack of skill, but a poor attitude. If we fail in our task our clients can again be knocked down and condemned to the failure they have become used to. The power to change lives is the motivation for being an ADI.

The Effects of Dyspraxia on Learning to Drive

Dyspraxia can result in wide-ranging characteristics and may be linked to a number of other conditions. The definition originates from **praxis** – practical, which coupled with **dys** – difficulty – is a brain processing disorder resulting in the poor organisation of the various stages involving thought, language and movement.

-It can be a result of an accident or Stroke – impairment, but what we are considering here is immaturity -a physical developmental condition.

-It may be determined before birth, with the term 'Clumsy Child Syndrome' previously being used to describe the characteristics. Similar difficulties can be observed following minimal brain damage which may then be classified as Mild Cerebral Palsy.

-Awkward, uncoordinated movements and erratic thought processes are typical and it may be possible to recognise the condition by observing the gait of the candidate, although any diagnosis must be avoided as these jerky movements could be caused by many other unconnected conditions.

-As many as 10% of the population will have learnt to function adequately with aspects of Dyspraxia, even though it may be undiagnosed or masked for other reasons. As it is not an illness but a physical dysfunction, they may explain it away by saying *"I am just clumsy"* and unless very severe they will not have regarded it as a disability.

-The instructor will encounter those who know they have problems but don't understand what they are, those who don't realise they have problems and maybe a few who actually have a diagnosis. Their difficulty in planning and organising their thoughts may have seriously held back their schooling and the confusing structure of some of the theory questions can seriously affect their ability to pass the Theory Test.

-Dyspraxia is also known as Developmental Coordination Disorder so they will have lived with the condition all their lives, but it may only be recognised as a problem when the complicated coordination and thought processes required for learning to drive are brought to the fore. Their self-esteem may have been severely affected as they have sought to make sense of an unrecognised and undiagnosed condition and have been bewildered by why they, as intelligent and capable people, cannot succeed. It may be more obvious if they have experienced delayed walking or speech development and required earlier help to clearly formulate words, but they may still question how this can have an effect on their learning to drive.

-These notes are to help ADIs and Examiners to understand the feelings that candidates with dyspraxia may be experiencing and through a deeper understanding of their needs we can all help to provide them with a positive test experience. As it is not an illness, but a neurological condition there is no cure, so the job of the instructor is to guide and assist in establishing the client's own coping skills in whatever unorthodox ways may be appropriate, rather than to impose a 'correct way,' and for the examiner to understand that the condition may make the candidate perform in a different way or manner. 'Hesitancy' for one person may be just taking necessary 'Care' for a person with dyspraxia and the reasons must be understood and catered for.

-They have often perfected excuses to avoid sport and just accepted being unable to be neat and tidy or to remember sequences and patterns which may have affected their mathematical ability to remember their tables, (dysnumerate). In other educational areas such as the free creative aspects of English, Music and Art they may have excelled, but now they have to come face to face with their suppressed demons. Not only do they not understand themselves, but they may find that their instructors also do not understand their thought processes or their actions, which just compounds their feeling of failure. To be effective, their learning must be in a developmental creative style rather than a directed formal one.

-Some will have found sports activities involving eye/ hand/foot coordination problematic, whilst others may have struggled with fine writing control or the sequential processing involved in dressing and tying shoe laces and buttons, using a knife and fork, opening bottles and cans or experienced confusion when using a mirror and trying to convert and understand a mirror image and may at first struggle with smooth steering. Rhythm will be difficult and they are unlikely to have been naturally able to ride a bike which is not really surprising if we consider the two sides of the brain struggling to work together with all the multitasking required.

-I am sure there will be those who can't see how these clients can or should drive safely, but all I can say is that they may be different to teach, but once they have learnt, with the new patterns being firmly established they can function as safely as other drivers. As with all disabilities there may be the rare occasions where one cannot drive because their problems are too severe, but if they have been given the chance, they can accept this because they have been provided with the opportunity and not told they cannot before they have tried. Each stage has to be taught and reinforced separately as they may find the transferral of skills learnt in one situation quite difficult to apply to another. "We did that last week" may not mean that they can do it this week, even though it is in a related situation.

-One highly literate woman explained that she viewed herself as a marionette where all her limbs functioned, but they all acted on their own and it was difficult to coordinate any movement together. Trying to do two things at once was impossible, so walking and carrying anything upstairs had to be avoided. The two sides of the brain may not be fluently linked so activities involving both hemispheres such as the T in R sequences can be difficult to process and each driving stage needs to be isolated so 'dry-steering' may be the only way to achieve this successfully. They have to learn one thing at a time. One asked in amazement *"you expect me to use two hands and two feet together?"* A manual car can be very demanding!

-They may have been 'mistakenly' classed as dyslexic because the poor coordination of the brain function can have caused problems with maths, reading, spelling and formal writing and they may cover up by blaming their 'stupidity' or their 'inability' to drive, instead of realising they have a different but recognised condition. If they understood the effects more, it would enable them to devise their own coping strategies.

-Instructors and examiners have to be able to recognise and understand why the candidate may be experiencing difficulties and to be aware they must not compound the problem by unnecessary requests or distractions. The instructor also must exercise extreme tact in addressing what is observed and in seeking background information, as it can be a very sensitive area to explore since frustration, anger, flash-backs and depression may be lurking just beneath the surface.

-I begin my research of their learning needs by asking about cycling, sport or art and the subjects they have selected to study. It is unlikely they will have chosen to progress with mathematics or even classical music where sequences and fine patterns are involved and they are unlikely to have been successful at the sports involving the quick coordination necessary for catching, throwing, kicking or balancing or with activities such as fine drawing or cutting with scissors. They may though be good at games such as snooker where time is available for the planning required or be quite artistic when relating to colour, texture, design and shapes and may informally play a musical instrument where they can be creative.

-As with all spectrums there will be many variations and the vast majority will not have had any formal diagnosis or classification attached to their condition since most likely it will have been viewed as a problem they would grow out of, or they will have subconsciously learnt daily coping and avoidance strategies. It may only manifest itself in a serious form when learning to drive or under the stress of a test, so for most sufferers a formal declared history is unlikely to be available.

-It is impossible to generalise, but those with the condition may cope by 'going into themselves', often becoming isolated or depressed, with males directing their intellectual skills in one specific area of interest or becoming frustrated and angry, whilst females may be overtly verbose about their stupidity and clumsiness or mask and excuse the problem by being 'dippy'. The most difficult job of the instructor is to be able to identify the hidden indications of such conditions and to be able to relate to and address the evidence without causing further stress. Their frustration may lead to a tendency to opt out of things that are too difficult, so don't be surprised if they give up or get frustrated or even stroppy, and try to be sensitive to understand the reasons why. Being misjudged is soul destroying and is what often happens to those with Hidden Difficulties.

-The examiner has even less time to make his assessment, but as they walk to the car he may get a clue by observing if the candidate moves in a jaunty manner or plodding ('walking in treacle') or if they accentuate their movements in the form of a skip. The run, skip or spring is used as a coping strategy to enable the jerky movement to become smoother.

-They may find it difficult to turn and change direction or struggle to use the key or open the bonnet or may be clumsy as they get into the car. It is more likely they will use an automatic car since they may have struggled with the processing required for manual driving and it is easier than having to admit they have a condition which sets them apart from their peers.

-The medical background of the condition is not usually relevant to driving, but dyspraxia is thought to be caused by an immature development of the neurones of the brain which transport information to the limbs, but even here there are differences of medical opinion and it is not in the brief of driving professionals to understand the causes. But an understanding of the effects is necessary and if the specific information-pathway is in any way compromised, then the resulting movements may become jerky or the initial stimulation may find another route or passage which results in delayed action. In extreme circumstances of stress the direction may short circuit which could result in extreme manifestations of panic and if not controlled could, in a driving context, be dangerous. An intention to turn right may be compromised by the message going in the wrong direction resulting in turning left with a right indicator showing.

-If the candidate has not already selected their preference for ID, then this is when the examiner must ask which method of ID they would prefer to use, since for most with dyspraxia, the sequential memory or the use of schematic diagrams could trigger panic and failure. It is to be avoided just like the warning on television for epilepsy sufferers that flashing lights will be on the news report. It is obvious that Schematic Diagrams must be a no-go area and if dyspraxia has not been declared, then in the interests of Road Safety the examiner must be able to understand that if they give sequential memory requests it could trigger confusion and any sudden change of direction to get them 'back on course' could be dangerous.

-The avoidance of stress is essential and unnecessary practice or the focusing on an error, can stimulate even more failure, which can then become ingrained. I have taught those who under stress have become muddled by intrusive instructions which has resulted in uncontrolled and 'violent' movements of the steering wheel or gear lever. Over time this spasticity has become less and less until it has no longer been an issue and they have been able to drive smoothly. The formal use of Q&A must be avoided as it is likely to cause a wipe-out of the mind and anyway the skilled instructor is able to assess the level of learning by observing, without the need for intrusive questioning. The application of knowledge is important, not the verbalisation or skill to be able to answer questions.

- An important aim of the instructor is to teach coping skills to help the client avoid unnecessary stress, but we must always be aware that test-stress could cause regression, which would not usually be manifest in their independent driving, so examiners also need to understand the issues so they can avoid creating increased stress through unclear requests.

-Candidates are sometimes failed because the examiner has misunderstood the motive behind the actions, rather than them having actually made an error which has resulted in any serious consequences and at times the error is directly as a result of the examiner's late instructions. It must always be remembered that it is the candidate's test and not the examiner's and candidates must be encouraged to drive using their own developed skills and coping strategies which they have learnt to enable them to become comfortably safe drivers. The examiner is there to observe a safe drive and candidates must not be seen as being necessarily wrong if they drive independently as they would when driving on their own, rather than acting under the examiner's specific requirements.

-Examples of this would be that if the mirror image confuses or overwhelms the brain, then its pedantic use could in certain situations be dangerous, but the use of general peripheral vision could achieve the same safe results and could in fact be the candidate's developed safe personal strategy; or in order to process a manoeuvre, there may be a delay as they struggle to organise the sequence in the correct order and so a gear change may be made earlier to enable their processing to have time to negotiate the junction safely. It may not be the ideal eco driving style, or what the examiner would do when he drove, but the question to be posed is whether it is actually wrong or dangerous.

-It is therefore vital that instructions are given clearly and in good time with the message reinforced through pointing, as they will find it difficult to remember more than one instruction at a time. The candidate should therefore not be marked down for making errors for a late gear change or for missing a mirror if the instruction has been given too late for them. It takes extra time for them to process the examiner's verbal instructions and in the time available, convert them into the required physical processes when acting under instructions, which is of course an alien intrusion into their normal independent safe driving process.

-To avoid the strategies used being misinterpreted it would help if we could all perceive these candidates as having a physical disability with which they are struggling to cope. It would then be easier to accept their 'misdemeanours', but life has never been easy for them because they appear to be 'normal,' and their actions can be misjudged by strangers especially under test-stress. Some of the best instructors and examiners for Specific Needs are those who have experienced difficulties themselves.

-I taught a dyspraxic woman with only a right arm, who still got confused with which way to turn since it was the brain-processing which was confused and not the physical process. Her intention was correct, but the muddle between the brain and the limb can be very distressing to the person concerned as they know what they intended to do, but the opposite action is the result. It is therefore important for them to learn how to manage the condition and its effects on their driving.

-As in this example the visible physical effects were easy to overcome, but the hidden thought processing can be very problematic especially on test, since it is not always clear how the information given to them will be processed and subsequently expressed. It can make them feel very embarrassed when their actions are contra to what they may have intended them to be especially when in front of a stranger in a position of authority. My explanation of the process is what we used to call going 'haywire' (or wire-wool) which is very difficult to unravel and one is not quite sure where the end will come out.

-A lifetime of coping strategies can become ravelled under the stress of a driving test, as happened when one of my candidates decided to negotiate a roundabout anticlockwise or when another tried to follow an arrow pointing the opposite way. Many Examiners and ADIs will have experienced those who have switched the right indicator and then turned left or got confused with what to do when they saw 30 and 40 written on the carriageway. The confusion would not normally happen, because they would drive within their comfort zone and avoid stressful test situations.

-The haze of the test can also cause the operation of switches and handbrakes to become greatly confused as the levers are pushed and pressed in all directions in an attempt to hopefully switch them on or release them. The positions up, down, backwards, or forwards are difficult words to interpret and in the early stages of learning they may lose position of the gear lever or gears and have to look at them. A test used to assess the balance of the brain following stroke is to see if they can point to the end of their nose with both hands with their eyes closed. Switches may become trial and error, so cars with fiddly multi-position switching systems should be avoided for such clients. A client's difficulty may not indicate an inability or a lack of experience, since they may be fine when using a less complicated system and may be able to overcome their problems when driving a suitable automatic car which gives them more time to think with fewer switches and levers to process. This can then enable them to establish a clear pathway within the brain.

-It may help our understanding of their difficulties if we consider the massive amount of brain power required to negotiate a roundabout even for the 'normal' driver and if we test ourselves by approaching one whilst verbally breaking down and talking through all the processes required; it is revealing just how much distance has been covered in such a short time and how distracted we can become by the exercise.

-The enormity of the problem is even clearer if we then think of the driver acting under alien instruction and stress and add on the extra time involved for the brain processing of the dyspraxic driver to listen to the instruction, register it, process and translate the meaning, before being able to select the appropriate pathway in the brain available for the action to take. Then compare this with the simple action of going down the known, pre-prepared route they would use on their daily independent commute.

-If we add into this scenario the dyspraxic candidate with English as a Second or Foreign Language then the problems become even clearer. 'Turn Left' has to be translated into their own language, transposed into the appropriate direction, before being converted into the required action, so it becomes clear how important the timing and clarity of the examiner's instructions are to the success of the client with dyspraxia.

-A poor short term memory can have surprising consequences and ADIs often talk about learners forgetting or day dreaming. I was giving directions to one lad as he approached a 'Give Way,' where he stopped unnecessarily and waited. I asked why he had stopped when the road was clear. He explained, *"If I press the clutch it wipes my mind of which way is right and which is left, so I have to stop and think."* This could be interpreted as 'losing concentration' as they struggle to synchronise the brain cogs, but in fact they are concentrating extra hard and not being lazy.

-Examiners must also be careful not to distract candidates by leading them off into pathways of conversation as they may not be able to switch back easily and quickly when required and under their own decision making process they would have chosen not to talk, but they answer because they believe that under exam conditions it may be deemed to be rude not to. They can appear to be listening, but the result is not what the instructor expects because they may hear an 'abridged' version which is actually different to what the instructor believes he has said.

-Some of us have witnessed the brains of our clients shut down when on tests and they have been faced with remembering a nine point sequence from a schematic diagram, but if we consider that they have no map reading ability, little sense of direction, have difficulty in distinguishing right from left and struggle to remember any sequence more than two, it is hardly surprising. I observed one examiner struggle to keep control when my candidate's mind 'crashed' on the seventh part of the sequence, but with sitting in the back, I had seen the wipe-out developing and would have aborted the requirement before the emergency arose.

-The main aspect of teaching these students is where possible to avoid, but also to teach how to cope with cognitive stress. The brain is an unbelievably complex organ which we are only just beginning to understand, so we have to train them to switch off from cognitive distraction or they may 'lose it' when overwhelmed.

-I have not covered ADHD in this book, but the condition can be similar to dyspraxia – difficulty in flexible thinking, a poor attention span, easily distracted and reacting to sensory stimulation without having the natural automatic controls. A horn can trigger a jerky response rather like the startle reflex spasm one might see from someone with Cerebral Palsy. They may be unable to sense the direction of an emergency vehicle and be only capable of doing one thing at a time properly, but they may still try to do many things at once. Overload can cause them to become unfocused and erratic, leading to poor concentration and a 'messy' performance, which may result in emotional outbursts and low self-esteem.

-If ADIs are concerned as to whether the learner is coping, then change the activity or reduce the load because they have a tendency to be erratic and have 'good and bad days.' Teach them to do things in stages so they are never overwhelmed. As soon as they begin to struggle, then move on because they don't learn if they are stressed. Increased cognition load can result in overload and you may not know what is on their mind to distract. I have sometimes spent part of a lesson discussing the personal problems of a client and afterwards questioned myself as to whether that was my role, but when I see them come bouncing out and eager for the next lesson because the load has been lifted and we can then put in a full session of hard graft, I realise that the learning only took place because we had resolved the problem and reached a stage where learning was possible.

The easiest way I explain the condition to myself is to say my computer has dyspraxic tendencies. Most of the time it works well; sometime it is smart and slick; then at other times I can hear it crackling under the load and I don't understand why. My solution is shut it down and switch it off. A few minutes later and it will be smart and on the ball again. Personally I cat nap for a few minutes and then I can also be back functioning well again, but if I don't switch off, I cannot work effectively any more than my computer can. Our customer's brains are just computers and we have to be able to understand them and occasionally be prepared to switch them off rather than overwork them. If your struggling learner shows a few of these symptoms then maybe they require more appropriate or different methods to teach them to drive independently.

The Effects of Dyslexia on Learning to Drive

-Prior to the introduction of Independent Driving I would have suggested that except for those who struggled with the Theory Test, few people with Dyslexia were actually prevented from driving because of their dyslexia. There are many famous dyslexic drivers who have attained professional success through their driving (Jackie Stewart) or in other activities such as dancing (Kara Tointon) where precise movement is required. I have also taught pupils in school with extremely severe dyslexia who have not experienced any problems when learning to drive.

-As Dyslexia became an 'acceptable' condition I found that people with other hidden conditions such as Dyspraxia used the term to get the help which would otherwise not be available to them. It does not really matter what the root is or term we use, but we need to be aware that Hidden Difficulties are very real and that instructors and examiners need to provide a different environment to enable these students to flourish and that the Specific Needs covered in this book are very real.

-The cross-over between the various terminologies used to describe similar conditions is irrelevant and in many cases has hindered the provision available especially if the specific charities are precious of the stated condition for which they advocate. Over the years this division has allowed government agencies to ignore the issues or to only latch onto what is cheap to provide.

-Immediately prior to the implementation of ID the DSA liaised with British Dyslexia Association, but neither party were able to appreciate the depths of the problems which may affect those with other hidden difficulties and so the meeting only produced one small armchair/ classroom perspective of the issues, instead of really researching the effects of all these conditions when driving at speed, in control of a moving car, under the stress of instruction and test. When most of the ideas discussed were shelved and only inadequate provision was made, the credibility of all involved was undermined. These vulnerable candidates were then left to struggle with the implementation of ID because it 'looked' as if something had been done to address their concerns.

-In many cases Dyslexia is a misnomer and therefore it is a misleading title which often results in the actual condition being dismissed because the student is able to read. This causes the student to feel at a loss because they cannot find a tag for their condition, or receive the help they require, so when they start to drive they may become defensive if the instructor seeks to discover if there is any dyslexia in the family.

-Much scientific research into brain function is now taking place and dyslexia is thought to be caused by different brain patterning and therefore the need to process information in different areas of the brain outside of the norm. This causes them to interpret stimuli in uncoordinated patterns. It is certainly not a disability because the ability to see life differently can stimulate incredible creativity, so it should not necessarily be deemed as a negative, but it should be recognised as a condition with support strategies being developed to assist functioning and to prevent society viewing it as a 'disability,' instead of being able to see and appreciate the different skills.

-There are estimated to be six million dyslexic people in Britain; 10% of the population with 4% having severe symptoms.

-A difficulty in Reading is not necessarily caused by Dyslexia as they may have other conditions or may have been inappropriately taught. Not all non-readers are dyslexic, although it is often used as a convenient term.

-Fluency in Reading does not necessarily preclude dyslexia as some people with dyslexic tendencies can read fluently because they are able to use other strengths of context and language to develop their reading skills.

-What has dyslexia got to do with driving? Many people have little understanding of how it could affect their learning, so if they struggle, they don't attribute it to their dyslexia or explain their difficulty to their instructor as they do not see it as relevant to learning a practical skill.

-The spectrum is very broad. Severe dyslexics may find they don't have problems, whilst others with only minor tendencies may have serious difficulties. They may have presumed that because they have learnt coping strategies within the classroom, then it will not affect their driving, but of course in a speeding vehicle they haven't the time to use their learnt strategies because they have to take time to evaluate the situation and engage the system and it is often then too late.

-<u>The Primary effect</u> may be a delay in processing. If the brain stimuli have to take a muddled pathway then it will take more time, so this delay is what affects drivers the most. The strategies they have developed become irrelevant in this new and dangerous environment and this causes stress, which at times can become very severe and manifest in a variety of ways. They must be helped to develop their planning skills to give them more time to decide and act safely and prevent being overwhelmed.

-<u>An Initial Solution</u> to find the time required can be obtained by first using an automatic car. This leaves time for the brain processing to kick in and to process what is happening. Owing to external pressures there may be a certain reticence so they need to be helped to analyse their condition to enable them to understand that it is not their difficulty in using the clutch or gears which has triggered this advice, but the need to smoothly process what is happening on the road. Once the reason is understood it is invariably accepted and they can always learn manual when they have developed natural driving skills and the stress has gone. Examiners and Instructors need to be aware that, although it is not always the case, those who present for test in Automatic cars may have additional undeclared difficulties and a dyslexic tendency may be at the root of their choice.

-<u>The Secondary effects</u> of a muddled mind can be confusion with the concept of right and left which takes time to sort out. In real life driving, careful planning using the Sat Navs arrows can help, but trying to puzzle out and interpret the verbal instructions of another can be quite problematic. Terms such as Nearside or Offside or Left and Right should be avoided unless accompanied by pointing, but 'My side' and 'Your Side' are terms which are usually understood and some feel happier to write left and right on their hand or wear a ring to identify a particular hand. This is very personal and the methods they have previously employed may be inappropriate. Children may have been taught to use the 'L' pattern formed by their left index finger and thumb, but the time taken to look would be inappropriate when driving. Precise pointing by the instructor is normally required and is the process which should be followed by the examiner.

-<u>Reading signs.</u> Essentially one learns to read by using a mixture of phonics, word recognition and contextual clues. Recognising and interpreting road destinations requires the specific skills of scanning to select the relevant sign, the identification of the shapes, letters and words from a mass of other information, translating it into a verbal word and interpreting it into a destination, then direction and the MSPSGL routine.

-If we consider how difficult this is for the 'normal' reader, it becomes obvious how complex and time consuming it is for the dyslexic brain to find the relevant pathways. Selecting the correct lane is further complicated when the brain with a right - left confusion gets muddled by similar shapes, colours and word patterns. There is so much information overload on approach to junctions which is then further complicated by the need to scan, select and download from different coloured signs whilst travelling at speed. It would help on test if Primary destination signs were chosen rather than being rushed to read Secondary signs with black print on a white background just before entry to the junction. - *"My reading isn't that bad, but with the added complexity of driving at the same time it breaks down. I end up going around roundabouts several times, scanning for my destination sign."*

-Some dyslexic readers have found that within a study context, the number of words on the page may become jumpy and muddled if printed on a stark white background so they may choose to provide a specifically coloured lens to reduce the contrast. Although this is not relevant to most, some may be more comfortable using tinted glasses when reading which will be particularly relevant for instructors when helping with the theory.

-As with any eye condition, what helps one will be a hindrance to another, so rather than instructors selecting for them, they may choose to provide their own personalised coloured transparency to cover the words. Sunglasses are often required to help them when driving and concerns have been voiced that the shiny yellow background at present in use on the schematic diagrams can detract from the clarity of the diagrams used.

-What effects do instructors encounter? I have had students totally panic at the thought of reading the words on signs, yet who seem to be able to read from a static page reasonably well. There are many reasons for this, but primarily they are flashbacks to school and the feeling of being stupid and the fear of being asked to read from the blackboard. One of the indicators used in the identification of dyslexia is those students who cannot take notes from the blackboard and feel imprisoned by the wall of words. They may be able to read, they may be able to write, they may even be able to spell, but the effort of the memory involved to transfer the information from one medium to another becomes problematic. This is why some dyslexic readers find they have difficulty reading similar shaped destinations on road signs when they have to look and read and then interpret the meaning and put it into action without having any contextual clues to make sense of it. They may have the same shape and same beginning and end with a similar medial pattern, but without any use of context they are indistinguishable and will confuse or delay the processing.

-These candidates would probably say they were able to read adequately because they would use contextual clues to 'cloze' the information being received. They may not even be regarded as having a Specific Need because of the coping strategies they had developed over many years, but they would still struggle with these words out of context. There is more to reading than barking at print and the cognition involved whilst on the move does not really kick in immediately since the brain power is being used for the process of the driving and recognising the sign, rather than comprehending the semantics of the information on it

-When undertaking ID, those dyslexics with a reasonable sequential memory would probably choose the Schematic Diagrams as the lesser of two evils, but they may refuse to look at the diagrams since this would further confuse because of their lack of scale, context, orientation and the number of shapes would just overwhelm them. I know some would regard it as 'teaching for test,' but as part of test preparation the ADI may need to give reading lessons of the specific signs and the place names they may encounter and practise the routes they may use.

-For those with both reading and sequential memory confusion then training needs to be undertaken in using Post-it notes or memory cards. For my own personal use I slot cards into my Sat-Nav holder on the dash board. I can then clearly see the route so they do not become the danger some examiners fear. I use arrows and numbers with circles as the best abbreviations because they don't need translating from R and L. It helps to state significant places; 'Station, Pub, Church or Supermarket.' It is vital to add scale and distance between junctions as this is the main complaint from 'normal' drivers about the confusion caused by the schematic diagrams since there is no indication of the distances between the turns.

-When struggling with word recognition, it is vital that precise wording is used. Take the direction which says **All Routes** is quite different to the one which says **All Other Routes**. To the dyslexic the double check required can involve travelling quite a few extra metres and they may then find they are too near the junction. Anyone doubting the level of these difficulties has only to drive in a foreign country to appreciate the navigational problems of scanning and reading jumbled letters or shapes. In real life these drivers would plan and learn their routes and make their own notes and just as the Word Processor has been the lifeline which has rescued many dyslexic Students, so have Sat-Navs been the lifeline for many dyslexic Drivers.

-The clarity of verbal instructions would benefit from being reinforced by pointing, since what may seem to be a clear direction can be misinterpreted. "I would like you to take the next turning left which is at the top of the hill." This would seem to be very clear, yet what is remembered is "at the top of the hill" and the turn left is forgotten, so when they reach the top of the hill and start to look for the left turn and then decide which direction is left, they have already driven past. It is quite revealing to ask what they thought the instruction was and it is even more important for the examiners to make their instructions perfectly clear.

-We cannot underestimate the psychological stress dyslexic students have been under for most of their lives. They try very hard to listen, but because it does not always make immediate sense or they do not respond immediately, the comments they are conditioned to hear are, "You are not concentrating," or "Listen to what I am saying," or "You would have known, if you had listened." "Pay attention" Even if these words are not used by ADIs the same attitude can often be unintentionally transmitted and received. Their coping strategies must be understood rather than criticised or regarded as a fault. They may wait a lot longer before acting because the processing takes longer to compute, but that should not be regarded as hesitation, but taking care.

-Many times I have to hold back from saying "Hurry up," and have to remind myself that it does not matter if they are not as quick as I may be as long as they are driving safely and rather than the instructor impulsively jumping in and taking action, they may need to carefully consider how much more time is needed to plan for situations. Teaching early action is particularly necessary as when Examiners apply the duals, candidates invariably say they were already taking action. It is therefore important to be taught how to avoid panicking the examiner into unnecessary braking.

-Dyslexia is a neurological condition and not laziness so we cannot expect them to do things in the same way as others. If they are disorganised or lose the study sheets we give them, it does not indicate laziness or a lack of care. In fact they may have tried extremely hard and feel embarrassed by their lack of memory. Low self-esteem may appear as lacking motivation, but we need to look beneath to see the real cause. That does not excuse the few who may play on their difficulties and sometimes a sharp retort is required, but for others a different solution can be found.

-I taught one youth who could not follow the analogue speedometer. Being unable to tell the time on an analogue dial is quite common amongst dyslexics, so I overcame the problem by fitting a satellite digital speedometer. I could easily have presumed he was deliberately not keeping to the speed, rather than asking and finding that it was because he could not understand the analogue system. They need to be taught the composition of a number plate since once they understand it they find it easier to read, but if it causes serious problems then provide a felt tip and pad or pointing grid so they can draw it for the examiner. These solutions are no different to the additions we use to help those with physical difficulties; extra mirrors, steering spinners or quick release handbrakes.

-Just as I can never remember people's names, it can be impossible for those with dyslexia to remember addresses or road names. *"Can you drop me off at my grandmother's?" "Where does she live?" "I will know when I get there!!"* We drove around until he recognised a shop and then he was able to recognise the road because driving is about doing and not about listening or remembering or following abstract directions.

-Always look 'beneath' and the 'hidden' will soon become clear.

An ADI's view of being Dyslexic

-Probably the biggest surprise I received after writing my first book were those ADIs who contacted me to thank me saying that not only had it changed their approach to their teaching, but it had also helped them to understand themselves and to realise that the problems they had struggled with all their lives may have had their roots in dyslexia. I did begin to wonder if this was the normal percentage of dyslexics in society or whether people with dyslexia were attracted to being driving instructors!

-In order to help other instructors understand the problem more deeply, an ADI wrote the following on a forum. I include it here as it gives us a succinct explanation from one of our own, to which many of us will be able to relate.

"I thought I would give some understanding into Dyslexia from what it is like to live with it. I love reading and am a fast reader and like big print books so I can clearly see every word. I don't understand nouns or verbs and took forever to understand vowels. I get letters mixed up b/d and z/s. I don't know my left from my right and had to practice which was my ring finger by putting a bracelet on my right hand so I knew the other one was the correct one. On lessons I just point and say" that way".

I won't talk to anyone I don't know, as when I am nervous I stutter and can say a random wrong word and feel stupid. I have no sense of direction, but once I have been to a place I can remember where to go. I can't remember street names or names and I don't know the streets around where I live. I have to think very carefully before I speak to make sure the right words come out.

My handwriting is awful and I am so happy that Word Processing exists and Spell Checking. I spell phonetically and it took me years to understand that Knife is spelled with a K and not a C. I have no grammar and don't understand it. I have no short term memory so the ID part of the test would fill me with panic. I have spent my life being told I was thick. I can't do maths and don't understand anything above adding. Everything takes time to understand. When I am going to a new place I spend time looking at the words of the place I will be going through so I can recognise them on the signs. Motorways are easy as I just have to know the number which I come off at. I hold maps in the way I am going.

I hope this has given everyone a bit of an insight into the ways Dyslexia can affect you. It affects everyone differently. Some are like me and quite severe, whilst others just get the odd letter mixed up."

The Effects of Autistic Spectrum Condition on Learning to Drive

-**ASC/ASD** covers a wide spectrum of characteristics which, (although a separate condition,) may be linked to dyspraxia. Many people who would appear to function quite normally have aspects of the 3 main classifications. It is not an illness, but an individual personality difference.

-**Autism:** severe cases will not be able to relate to other road users well enough to enable them to drive safely. Those who do may appear to be extremely shy or refuse to speak, (elective mutes) make odd sounds and only feel complete within their own world. The car environment allows them to be relaxed and become competent drivers and can enable them to function normally, comfortably and safely within their own metal box.

-**Aspergers:** often highly intelligent, avid researchers, incredibly knowledgeable within a specific narrow field of interest, but may lack understanding of what would normally be recognised as basic life matters. They can switch from adult to childlike behaviour and become stressed by the unfamiliar. They may be very verbose and appear to be superior, but detached from reality and will be happier in adult 'sensible' company. As they see life differently they enrich all our lives with their humour and use of language and if guided correctly they can learn to drive appropriately.

-**Semantic Pragmatic Disorder:** a difficulty in understanding language in normal usage. They can experience severe problems with complex Theory Questions and will require detailed explanations with which they may argue, because to their way of thinking, the answer is illogical. The knowledge will be there, but the required answer may not be forthcoming, although a rational explanation may be expressed. They may however not understand why their 'correct' answer is unacceptable.

-Having developed Social Skills they may present as 'normal', but Q&A is often irrelevant and may cause panic or mental freezing as they try to work out what the question means and what response is required. They find it difficult to fully understand through the medium of speech and may take words literally without the ability to accept subtle hints or any understanding of innuendo. If language is clear and direct they can function very competently in practical activities such as driving.

-Test candidates are unlikely to be prepared to state their condition on their application as it is personal to who they are as people and they would not see themselves as being abnormal or disabled. In fact they would perceive the other people to be different for not being able or prepared to accept their particular characteristics. This may have led to bullying, withdrawal and self harm. They can behave in fixed and formulated patterns as there is a right and wrong way to behave, so if others are in the wrong, then they are the ones who should make the necessary changes and rather than be impetuous, they will wait until the situation is resolved. It is often black and white. Examples on test-

-A candidate turning right at a roundabout found his exit lane partially blocked on both the right and left, but leaving a gap in the middle. He waited for one car blocking his way to reverse to allow his free passage. The reason for this extra care was not appreciated by the examiner so he failed for positioning.

-Another candidate was about to begin to reverse round the corner when a car approached so he correctly waited. The driver turned into his drive, got out, opened the boot, collected his belongings, opened the door of the house, walked in and closed the door. The candidate knew he could now continue as the danger was over. He passed with a hesitation d/f as the examiner said, "I realised he was a bit different".

-Face to face discussion is difficult, but they are also unlikely to be able to converse by phone, since the social clues are absent. The suggested phone call from the DSA seeking information would be inappropriate for them and bizarre or amusing conversations can often develop on lessons. In an attempt to break the ice at the start of a test one examiner asked,

"What shall I call you?"	*Call me what you like.*
"What do you friends call you?"	*I don't have any friends.*
"What does your mother call you?"	*It depends -----*

As they walked to the car a somewhat inappropriate question was asked,
"Oh you have Aspergers. How does that affect you?"
Well Aspergers is a broad spectrum condition, so it would take a long time to explain the number of effects it has on me.

During the test,
"Well it is not as bad as you expected is it?
You have not given me the result yet!!

-The initial conversation can often be the indicator for the examiner to realise he will require empathetic understanding to conduct the test in an appropriate way. Candidates are unlikely to make normal eye contact, often looking down at the floor, but on the other hand may scrutinise the examiner's face as they attempt to comprehend and relate. In order to adequately test their driving ability, the examiner will need to avoid distraction and give clear precise instructions reinforced by pointing.

-A choice of ID must be offered as for many the Sequential Memory Test has proved to be actually dangerous owing to the brain being overwhelmed by the task of memory, rather than it being fully available to be used for safe driving. On tests I have observed both total panic and those where the switch to concentrate on the traffic has wiped the mind of the required sequence. This resulted in the candidate's embarrassment as the examiner was required to take a detour to get back on track.

-The feedback is that they find the schematic diagrams a distraction, and believe it safer to try to remember the sequence rather than look and be distracted. They have to be in total control of their driving, so if they do not see the purpose of something or it disturbs their concentration, they will have learnt to use avoidance strategies to cope with the distraction. This is a major part of teaching them to drive safely where they learn to prioritise and switch, so it is an anachronism for them then to be tested on their short term sequential memory recall under the stress of test.

-An interesting aspect is that when a pattern is fully established, it will then become permanent and they will remember the route in great pedantic detail, (even commenting on what the person at the traffic lights was wearing or the breed of dogs) In a known location and with practice they will be able to follow a route completely accurately or when following Sat Nav instructions, so truly independent driving will not cause them any problems. Reading is not usually difficult and they may be able to learn rote facts such as Railway Timetables or detailed road routes and destinations, but their difficulty lies in their relationship with the verbal instruction and the need to interpret its meaning so as to remember in the short term. This may be an impossible hurdle to overcome and why they require to be given the destination signs to read when on test.

-I asked an examiner why he had chosen to give a 9 part (4+3+2) Sequential Memory Test to a highly intelligent candidate with declared Aspergers and was taken aback by the reply *"I did not think he would be able to read the destination signs as Aspergers is like Dyslexia."* This comment triggered these guidelines as I realised that examiners are doing their best, but they are uninformed and the DSA emphasis on Dyslexia has in some cases blinkered their minds to the other Hidden Disabilities.

-When concern for these candidates is raised, the official response is 'they are able to ask the examiner for reinforcement', but asking help from a stranger is not something they would ever do in real life, so to ask an official test examiner in a position of power to repeat the instructions would be too stressful or even impossible. There are those who would be more able to write a letter than ask a face to face question. To query an examiner would be beyond their communication and emotional skills.

-In theory, provision has been made for these disorders, but in practice it has not been complied with and the struggle for these candidates to remember the sequences has proved to be both torturous and dangerous. *'this could be by asking you which method you prefer - following traffic signs or a series of directions (a maximum of three), which are supported by a diagram. In some cases this may be shortened to just two directions.* (DSA guidelines)

-Their difficulty in performing this new part of the test does not of course imply they are not perfectly capable drivers, but that it is inappropriate to test them by using these methods. They may happily use technology since those with these difficulties usually relate to inanimate objects more easily than to people, or they may use Post-it notes, not only to trigger their memory, but also to prevent the memory from being overwhelmed by the task of attempting to remember when the traffic conditions require their full concentration. I am sure I am not the only ADI who uses a Sat Nav and Post-it notes and know that I would struggle on a test to remember and recall three sequences of instructions whilst coping with the changing traffic conditions.

-By nature they are inflexible, so in order to learn to drive safely they must be exposed to how to cope with situations which are constantly changing. The direct retort *"You said!"* should not be taken as an aggressive response, but a desire to comprehend that what you said in one context is now different because the situation has changed. They may appear to be rude, but *"Got it! Got it!"* means they now understand. If the instructor repeats something they already know, or uses 'mirror' as a one word prompt, they may receive an aggressive *"I know! I know!"* What the instructor means is 'you are not doing it correctly,' but 'shorthand/shortspeech' is difficult for them to interpret and it may receive a hasty retort which must not be interpreted as a refusal to listen or learn.

-There are not many things a person with Aspergers cannot achieve, but there are those with Semantic Pragmatic Disorder who have been prevented from passing the Theory Test because of the DSA's insistence on it being a memory-based test rather than knowledge-based. Exasperated parents often say, *"When I rephrase the question, he knows the answer."* The refusal to allow candidates to ask their readers for explanations of the more complex questions, (as they would be able to in education exams) discriminates against them because of their disability. They usually score highly on the HPT and it is not through lack of practical ability that they are prevented from driving because as long as they are understood and taught in a different way, they can learn to drive safely. If the testing is done according to their strengths and their learnt strategies, rather than facing them with what they cannot do, then they can legally become integrated into the driving community.

-The smartly dressed young man with the social skills who presents for test may mask these ASC characteristics which the examiners now need to be experienced enough to identify. Otherwise they may continue to make the wrong judgements which have become more obvious since the introduction of ID and desire of instructors to sit in and observe tests.

-ASC covers a wide spectrum of the most interesting and creative people who have much to contribute to our society and they must be recognised as valuable in their own right and have an equal opportunity to attain a licence through differentiation. Their interpretation and understanding of life is just as acceptable as the formulated bureaucratic one that the Civil Servants expect them to pedantically follow, but this concept seems difficult for both sides to comprehend.

How can we teach those with Hidden Difficulties?

-Some comments from instructors about those with Hidden Difficulties are: "they don't remember what I tell them"; "they ignore simple instructions"; "what they can do one day they have forgotten by the next"; and *"they do exactly the opposite from what I tell them."* On the other hand the complaint made by their learners is: *"he keeps telling me things and expecting me to listen and understand, but I don't learn like that."* The problem lies in them being 'asked to do', rather than being 'allowed to do' what comes naturally to them, even if it is different from what the Instructor expects them to do.

-Is it a difficult learner or the instructor having difficulty?

-The ADIs often believe they have to 'teach' instead of facilitating students to 'learn' in whatever way is best for them and examiners believe they have to 'examine' rather than provide opportunities for candidates to drive to the best of their ability. I term this 'Developmental Driving'-when learners develop their own style of comfortable safe driving under the instructor's guidance rather than listening to what he wants them to do and the examiner allowing them to show what they can do, rather than expecting them to do what they cannot, or don't actually need to do.

-It is true that we cannot 'teach' some clients, but that does not mean they cannot <u>learn</u> and we can help them to learn by exposing them to as many hazards and diverse situations as possible so that they learn experientially. We can guide them to develop what they already have established through the many experiences they have had before they come to us and develop those skills through informal repetition. They learn through the <u>drip, drip of experience</u> and can succeed to drive independently in their own way, but honed by the instructor. It may be impossible to predict how they will perform the test, but it will be possible to say they will be safe considerate drivers. They don't need any questions or analysis or words. It is development through routine and this is how they live their lives; to the same shops and to the same workplace. They don't require the complexities we try to feed them or what we demand from them. Familiarisation and a comfortable environment desensitises them from any panic. In rural areas where there are no buses, learning to drive is an important factor in halting the vicious cycle of unemployment.

-The instructor cannot aim for a set level of skill- perfection because he will not get it, but the clients will reach a satisfactory level where they will be able to drive safely and defensively. If they are set a standard they will not be able to reach they will fail in despair, but if they are allowed to develop they will become independently safe competent drivers. If they are expected to remember, then the mind will shut down because they know they cannot retain the information, but if they get continuous exposure, then the more proficient they will become and so will become relaxed and the learning will be more rapid. It is what I call "Top-Down Teaching" where the pathways in the brain are developed from the known or instinctive actions and then stimulated by the new challenges.

-Although we normally think SN is about teaching the slower learner, driving difficulties are not necessarily anything to do with intelligence and may in fact be just the opposite, as lateral thinkers may make good drivers, but it may not be conducive to passing the test. We hear of prominent celebrities who have taken many attempts to pass, but they have become perfectly capable drivers when they have been allowed to drive in their own way and when they have achieved their success they feel able to go public about their struggles. The quick thinkers may find it more difficult to pass a set test than the pedantic plodders and denial of a problem is often a major cause of failure of the highly intelligent.

-If one is academically able it is hard to recognise one may have a diagnosable condition, so candidates with these problems are often reluctant to declare their difficulties on their Test Application. One method I use to help overcome a specific hurdle is to provide the auto where they can practise without overload. They may never have accepted driving an auto if they felt I was suggesting they had a problem and implied they could not cope with manual, but that is not how I explain it. The auto is just a ladder to assist their learning development so they accept its use without question and many choose to stay with it.

-If candidates will not declare their difficulties it does mean both the instructors and the examiners will require extra skills to ensure the correct decisions are arrived at. They need to be able to understand Hidden Difficulties as well as the Stated Disabilities.

Practical Test Provision

-The DSA has always provided for those with Physical 'Special Needs', but in recent years ADIs who specialise in clients who struggle, have tried to raise an awareness of those with 'Specific Needs' in an attempt to bring the DSA in line with accepted Educational Provision and that acknowledged and provided for in the Workplace.

-The 1981 Education Act stated that not only physical, but also learning difficulties had to be identified, recognised and provided for through legal 'Statements'. Implementation of these Statements was part of my previous career and is at the root of my deep interest in calling for the DSA to provide for all those with Specific Needs in line with Educational practice. I believe it is now time for an independent report into the provision for all drivers with SN; not only learners, but also the increasing number of disabled drivers and those aged over seventy.

-Although the recognition of Dyslexia has now become acceptable, Specific Needs were still not considered within the recent DSA Consultation and there seems to have been little understanding or provision made as Dyslexia often has little effect on those learning to drive. The implementation of ID has however brought the whole issue of other Hidden Difficulties to the fore and there have been a number of cases where those with Specific Needs have been disadvantaged through the form of ID they have been asked to undertake. Discussions have now taken place to ensure that, as far as possible, candidates are not required to do what they would find impossible or dangerous.

-Those with declared SN are now allowed to choose the form of ID they would prefer and if it is thought that extra time will be required to prepare their route, they can elect for a double slot when booking. However undeclared SN are still excluded from this provision.

-*'The intention of Independent Driving is not to disadvantage anyone or any element of society, to that end such a candidate may choose either ID method that best suits with any additional help (i.e. Post-it notes) A candidate with Special Needs etc. can select whichever means of independent driving they would prefer.'* (DSA)

-If candidates find reading and scanning signs difficult, they can elect for schematic diagrams; if they have sequential memory problems, then they are able to use the destination sign-reading exercise, but if they struggle with both, they are allowed to make their own Post-It notes to which they can refer to trigger their memory. Even if they would normally use technology in their daily commute, they are still not allowed on test to use verbal instructions via Sat Navs or visual mobile phone mapping.

-As most Specific Needs are hidden, the identification of need has put an impossible responsibility on the skills of the Examiner. It is therefore the task of the ADI to make sure examiners are fully aware of the client's needs. Following a number of errors I have negotiated with my Centre Manager to e-mail the candidate's requirements before test and to explain to the examiner the needs of the candidate. This would be frowned upon by some, so I would not advise it without prior authorisation.

-The problem lies in the fact that the majority of candidates do not want to be classed as having Specific Needs, or do not have a specific diagnosis and there are others who actually object to receiving positive discrimination. It is also surprising that people having driving difficulties do not always equate it with their accepted sequential memory problems. It may be the same root, yet they presume that because they are academically capable they will therefore not have any difficulty with driving. Of course they may not, but often they do. The examiner is then in the unenviable situation of having to determine the best way to examine their strengths, but through lack of knowledge they often get it wrong.

-Post-it notes have been refused on the grounds of perceived danger and lack of time, so examiners prefer double slots organised at the booking stage. The simplest way is to declare 'dyspraxia' since 'dyslexia' and other Hidden Difficulties only trigger a single slot, but 'dyspraxia' is categorised as a physical problem so double time will be given for the planning.

-It would help if every candidate were offered their preference when booking as it would remove any negative or positive discrimination whilst maintaining the integrity of the test. Why this is not acceptable has never been justified, but sometimes the simplest answer is the most difficult to effect, so my solution through education seems to be one way forward.

Theory Test Provision

-This is not the place to go into details re the would-be learners who are prevented from actually getting to the driving test stage owing to their lack of academic prowess. We have all seen the dream taken from them, and the light of hope fade from their eyes, but there are little-known provisions available which they can access. It is rare for them to experience problems with HPT as they usually attain high scores, but they do struggle with the MCQ where memory and confusion are paramount.

-If clients book by phone, they can ask for extra time and to use Headphones with English (or a number of other languages) read to them.

-If they send a Statement of Educational Needs, (a legally binding document) or a report written by an Ed. Psychologist stating their requirements, or a LA form stating their disability, this should be enough to enable them to receive an actual person to read the questions to them.

-If they do not have any formal recognition of their need, they will require a letter from their doctor or educational establishment which they will usually have to pay for. The draw-back to having a reader is that they are only allowed to read the question and are not allowed to explain anything, nor answer questions about the wording and this can lead to misleading clues being taken from the reader. This worry is especially pertinent if the client struggles with Semantic Pragmatic Disorder which is an inability to understand the fine meaning of the language used in the test.

-If they have a physical difficulty which prevents them from holding the mouse or using the touch screen, they can arrange to bring their own adaptation to fit to the monitor. This has to be pre-arranged as not all monitors have suitable ports available.

-Applying for Special Needs provision is not made easy and the booking system can be frustrating even for professional people to undertake, so if the candidate has SN it is advisable for the ADI to book it for them, but make sure you have all relevant documentation to hand. Like all call centres your experience may be good, but to get what your client needs you may have to insist on speaking to a Special Needs Advisor. It is usually a case of a lack of understanding as to the correct category to put the client's needs, rather than the provision not being available.

-The sifting out of would-be drivers by the MCQ has been a long standing issue since it causes problems to so many of the less academic applicants and also to those who think in a different way to how the questions are worded. It excludes those candidates who have difficulty in studying in a logical and sequential way without becoming distracted and the instructor must be able to see beyond the 'lazy' label with which they may have been tagged at school and which will have compounded their difficulties in trying to remember facts in isolation. In real life they are perfectly able to understand and apply in a practical context.

-These pupils may have a vast source of information, but not be able to put it into a logical and meaningful order to answer the MCQ and these difficulties can lead to frustration and problems with self esteem which can further lead to either withdrawn or disruptive behaviour. There is a lot to overcome and a huge responsibility on ADIs and the DSA to try to understand and address the issues to help them to succeed where formal education and driving instruction has failed them in the past.

-I have taught lads under Sp. Ed. who have had a deep knowledge of cars, roads and driving and what they have learnt on their own, which has stimulated their interest, but have rejected the formal education reliant on memory as being impossible for them to retain as many of the theory questions are. We must therefore accept Driving Development as the way forward in order to develop their skills at their own level and need, rather than to impose inappropriate methods and assessments from above.

-ADIs who have taught those with Aspergers will appreciate their encyclopaedic knowledge of roads, transport and history and also the struggles they have to answer some of the MC Questions. On an ID section the examiner checked to see if the candidate with Aspergers had remembered the town he was supposed to be travelling toward. He immediately gave the route number he was following even though it had never been mentioned. He knew his way, but it was not the way the examiner had given him. This lad had seriously struggled with the theory, but he knew it in practice. I fear that the new Theory Test format will still favour those with memory skills and discriminate even more against those who are knowledgeable, but whose brain may be wired differently.

How do YOU respond?

-Many readers will have bought this book after having read my previous ones which went into more detail regarding teaching ideas and specific successes; but I also realise that some will be considering these matters for the first time and that the comments I have made may be regarded as quite revolutionary or outside the parameters suggested in your training. There will be others who have been questioning, 'is there another way?' but have wondered if it would be acceptable and what it should be: of-course that depends on the development of your personal skills as a teacher and the relationship between you and your clients.

-Some new instructors would regard their job to be working to a set syllabus to train learners to perform in the way they would act until hopefully they turned into replicas of themselves. It therefore comes as quite a surprise when a number of their trainees don't learn that way and they wonder why. Just as we cannot tell our trainees how to drive independently, no one can tell the teacher how to teach independently. It is not dependent on academic study or a set course or philosophy since the skills you require are not only client specific, but will change during each lesson. The key question to ask is whether both you and your students are succeeding and enjoying the lessons since many learners are pushed into traditional forms of instruction which overwhelm them. If they are not succeeding or enjoying the lessons then something needs addressing.

-One aspect of my work is to re-train drivers following brain injury and the problems they encounter are very similar to those that our learners with hidden difficulties experience. There may be some part of the brain which does not operate in quite the same way as we would expect, but exciting research into brain function is revealing more and more about how the brain can seek out new pathways and directions in order to cope with the problems and begin to work adequately again. Until recently the concept that one could learn to see by using other senses such as the touch or hearing would have seemed to be science fiction, so we should not dismiss our candidates who struggle, but rather seek out exciting and creative ways to help them to succeed.

-The more experience I have had as a Driving Instructor the more I have observed the vast differences in drivers' skill, aptitude, attitude, experience, health, perception, reaction speed, and the ability to predict and problem-solve. I realised that irrespective of intelligence or education, many drivers do not see or do what I would think was common sense; not deliberately or because of stupidity or road rage, but because they do not perceive the situation in the way I do or have the experience to predict, or the ability to find the same solutions.

-The skill level of some of our candidates may not be as brilliant as others, but we can still help them to compensate by teaching care for others, awareness and defensive driving whilst exposing them to many wider experiences. The serious accidents on our roads are not usually caused by those with problems, but by those whose attitude is poor or who believe they are highly skilled. It is therefore also necessary to educate our naturally skilled drivers to understand that they need to allow more time for drivers who are less skilled than they are. As part of my Pass Plus course I encourage my higher skilled drivers to experience driving with hand controls as it teaches them to be more aware of the hidden needs of others who share the road with them. All strands of society are on our roads and all drivers need to be taught to be aware of and to accept each other's needs. There has to be a place for all, rather than just those who fit a pre-determined standard on a given day.

-As part of the development of your work as an instructor I would encourage all readers to research further into the three conditions covered in this book. I have only just touched upon the spectrums and there are of course many other neurological dysfunctions and hidden difficulties we may encounter which do not fit the standard teaching template. Some may be temporary and caused by trauma which if given time and the required help the brain can heal. We must not 'write them off', but instead try as many different ways as possible to help them achieve the same as those we teach whom we would regard as being 'normal.' If you decide to specialise in this area of work you will not be disappointed as it is both fascinating and extremely rewarding, especially when you see lives changed because of your interest, care, knowledge and developing expertise. *John P Brown 2011*

Notes from an ADI whose son has Aspergers and Dyspraxia

- Tend to be rules-based and react badly to people who break the rules.

- Because they love rules, once they have learnt mental checklists they will stick rigidly to them, but be careful that they are not just going through the motions - Are they looking AT the mirror or IN the mirror? What have they seen?

- Love routines. Strongly dislike change. Need to know what is coming next before they have started the current activity. Need to have a structure and know where they are in the structure. Stick to a regular lesson slot and try not to cancel.

- Because they dislike change - introduce each new challenge as an extension of something already met rather than something new.

- Easily distracted - you need to find really quiet places to start with, free from as many other distractions as possible to help them to concentrate.

- Hard to copy what you demonstrate. If you show them how to hold and turn the wheel then they will try to copy, but it will look nothing like what you did. There is a real difficulty in relating what they are doing with their hands and feet to what they have seen someone else do. They really need to try for themselves rather than being shown what to do.

- With dyspraxia expect harsh use of pedals as they find it hard to control feet.

- Take it slowly; allow them plenty of time to get used to you and lots of time to practise each step so as to build up confidence.

- They tend to have unrealistically high expectations and then be unreasonably hard on themselves when they don't achieve them. They can give up very quickly – "I just can't do it!" so help them to set goals in smaller steps.

- They find it difficult to see things from other people's perspectives. **Avoid** asking questions like: "What will that other driver do?" "What would happen if we were coming the other way down the road?" "How much can the other driver see?"

- You need to put them into the exact situation you want to ask them about. Anything else will lead to intense frustration for both the pupil and for you!

- They tend to avoid eye contact which can make communication difficult.

- You will probably need to come up with some strategies for getting the eyes moving more specifically in order to develop effective observations. I play a game to get them looking into driveways and side roads where they have to count all the red cars they see and have to have recognised them before I do. When they get good at that we discuss other red things we should be looking for- red traffic lights, red brake lights and then we move on to red traffic signs and eventually I get them scanning around looking for everything they need to look for as drivers.

- It can be hard work as they can become very focussed on the particular thing which has their attention and then find it hard to divide their attention e.g. they could become fixated by the rev counter and not watch the road because at that particular time they are interested in the rev counter and so become blinkered to everything else. It is important to teach them to prioritise what they should be focussing on.

These are pointers from my experiences both as an ADI and a parent. Aspergers is a broad diagnosis and as with all pupils, everyone is different.   Mike Ward @ www.Driving-lessons.net

Concerns regarding this system of ID

Those who have read my previous books will know I advocate that Driving Independently may be the only safe way for learners with SN to drive, so ever since the DSA plans for ID were first made public I have tried to ensure that the form of ID implemented would be relevant and applicable to those with Specific Needs. A number of experienced ADIs aimed to make sure that our two Governments would be fully aware of the issues so as to prevent anyone being disadvantaged. Unfortunately, practice has indicated that this experience and advice was largely ignored and the success claimed has been mostly due to flexible and understanding examiners.

In 2008 the DSA consulted with its stake holders re the future of the Driving Test and as soon as the Consultation was opened I personally made representation to advocate for this group of learners to make sure the needs of those with Hidden Difficulties were both recognised and understood. It was particularly important to push for recognition since those with memory difficulties had only recently been disadvantaged by the raising of the number of MC Theory Questions from 35 to 50 involving an increase in memory recall rather than practical knowledge.

During my discussions with senior DSA staff I became aware of both their intransigence, but even more concerning, a lack of understanding of the issues and when I publically raised SN with the CEO, I got the distinct impression that the form of ID proposed was already a done deal and that those with Different Abilities were not to be considered as it would 'affect the integrity of the test'.

When the opportunity arose to take part in the ID trials, I knew that the 21% the Government stated had SN would not be fairly represented, so I submitted four candidates with differing needs to ascertain if my predictions of their difficulties would have any foundation. The evidence indicated that whilst some had problems with the sign reading, others struggled with the Sequential Memory Recall Task and the use of the Schematic Diagrams. I had to physically intervene on two occasions which reinforced my view that any unnecessary cognitive distraction, especially when coupled with overload, could be dangerous.

As it was not a Test, the examiner sat behind with the ADI accompanying the client in the front passenger seat. The instructor therefore had the best overview of the trials, but their professional feedback was not sought. I contacted the Transport Research Laboratory who were undertaking the research and was informed that their research was not really independent as they were under a DSA brief and not in a position to step outside of that brief to accept the observations of the instructors or to make the understanding of SN more representative. Subsequent analysis of the evidence would indicate disturbing gaps in the research and its interpretation.

MPs and Government Ministers refused to address the issues and avoided their responsibility by passing any correspondence back to the DSA, so that even letters to the PM ended up with the CEO. I did begin to doubt both our Democracy and Parliamentary system. Shortly before the launch of ID misleading information was published and the realisation dawned that there could be room for a legal challenge under the Disability Discrimination Act. The DSA decided to have a meeting with the British Dyslexia Ass, but the 'experts' were not practising ADIs and only represented one section of those with Hidden Difficulties, so the discussions were able to be sidetracked. The needs of those with disabilities had now been 'officially' considered with the tangible result being a cream background to the Schematic Diagrams.

DSA officers now refused to communicate and were intent on pushing ID through without listening to or addressing the issues and so again misleading information was released which could not be challenged. The responsibility for its success was heaped on the shoulders of the examiners, who had received little, if any extra training to help them to cope with clients with Hidden Difficulties, and on the reticent candidates to ask for reinforcement of the required memory route. Even senior staff did not fully understand what was being proposed, so it was no surprise that there were serious problems at the coal face. As many ADIs observed from the back seat, these were fundamental faults and more than just teething troubles, so now we are attempting to shut the door after the horse has bolted.

This book is aimed at redressing any gaps in understanding through **information** and **education**, but until learning to drive is regarded as 'an Educational process,' those who don't understand or don't care will be able to invoke the 'integrity of the test' as the excuse for not recognising or for not providing for those who need specific help to assist their learning. After 30 years of legal **inclusion** within Education, it is time that **access** to the Driving Test was given integrity for all, since driving seems to be sliding towards the **exclusion** of those either less academic or with hidden difficulties, whilst the closure of rural bus routes is for many making the need to drive a necessity.

Even if using unorthodox methods, driving independently in a safe and responsible manner is the only way forward for those with Hidden Difficulties. The introduction of ID has been an excellent development for the majority of candidates, but we must avoid any cognitive distraction by the system the examiner is required to use. To make it more acceptable, without there being any positive or negative discrimination, it is essential that every candidate be offered a choice of the method of ID they require. In fairness to all its candidates, the DSA cannot continue to cling to the present oxymoron of 'directed independence'.

John P Brown. February 2011   www.drivingincludesu.co.uk